Th

REV. JUDE WINKLER, OFM Conv.

Imprimi Potest: **Michael Kolodziej, OFM Conv.**, Minister Provincial of St. Anthony of Padua Province (USA)
Nihil Obstat: **Rev. Msgr. James M. Cafone, M.A., S.T.D.**, Censor Librorum
Imprimatur: ✠ **Most Rev. John J. Myers, J.C.D., D.D.**, Archbishop of Newark

The Nihil Obstat and Imprimatur are official declarations that a book or pamphlet is free of doctrinal or moral error. No implication is contained therein that those who have granted the Nihil Obstat and Imprimatur agree with the contents, opinions or statements expressed.

God Creates the Angels

EVERY Sunday when we go to Mass, we profess our faith in God when we say the Creed. This is a very old prayer that was written to remind us of what all Christians believe.

One of the things that we proclaim in the Creed is that God created everything, including all things that we can see, and even those things that we cannot see.

What do we mean when we say that God created the things that we cannot see? You might think that we are talking about the air, or maybe atoms that are too small for us to see.

God did create those things, but that is not really what we are talking about. The unseen things that God created are the spirits—creatures that exist without a body that we can touch or see.

We are especially talking about the Angels, spiritual creatures who serve God. They do not have bodies like we do. They are pure spirit.

Angels carry God's Word to us and our needs and prayers to Him.

Some Angels Rebel

GOD created the Angels to be good and to do His Will. Long ago, however, before Adam and Eve were created, some of the Angels refused to do that. Those Angels rebelled against God.

The leader of the rebellion was an Angel named Lucifer. We hear about him in various places in the Bible and from other ancient stories that have been passed down to us.

Lucifer was a beautiful Angel. In fact, only God was more beautiful than he was. His name means the "light bearer," for he radiated God's glory. Yet, that was not good enough for him. He did not want to be second best.

Lucifer rebelled against God. He convinced a number of Angels to join in his rebellion.

St. Michael, the Archangel, served as God's representative to defeat Lucifer and his evil Angels. They never really had a chance, for God's goodness and love are so much more powerful than any evil.

God cast Lucifer and the rebel Angels into hell.

In the Garden of Eden

WE meet two Angels in the first pages of the Bible during the story about another rebellion, the rebellion of Adam and Eve.

God created the world and everything in it. He presented it to Adam and Eve and gave them permission to use it for their needs. He asked them only not to eat the fruit of the Tree of the Knowledge of Good and Evil that was in the middle of the Garden of Eden.

The devil tempted our first parents. He got them to disobey God by convincing them to eat the fruit of the Tree of the Knowledge of Good and Evil.

Even though Adam and Eve had sinned, God still loved them. Yet, He had to punish them. God cast out Adam and Eve from the Garden of Eden. They would not enjoy the fullness of God's peace again until Jesus died on the Cross for us. We will not enjoy the Garden of Eden again, in fact, until we are with God in heaven.

God placed two Cherubim at the gates to the Garden. The Angels remind us that sin shuts us out.

Abraham Welcomes Three Guests

WE meet Angels in the story of Abraham. One day he was sitting by his tent when he saw three strangers approaching. Since Abraham was living in the desert, he was expected to take care of them (for in the desert there is so little to eat and drink that a person might not make it if people did not show him hospitality).

Abraham did not realize that his guests were God and two Angels. He fed them well, and showed them much respect and generosity.

God rewarded Abraham and his wife, Sarah, for their goodness. He promised them that by that time the next year, they would have a son. God fulfilled His promise and their son was named Isaac.

God's two companions then traveled on to the city of Sodom. There people did not show hospitality to the Angels. God therefore decided to punish the city and the cities around it by burning them to the ground.

Yet, the two Angels saved Lot, Abraham's nephew, and his family, for his kindness.

The Birth of Samson

A NOTHER time an Angel appeared to a woman of Israel whose husband's name was Manoah. The Angel promised her that she would have a son.

These were very difficult times for Israel. They were constantly being attacked by their enemies. Every time they would plant a crop, their enemies would come and either steal it or destroy it. Israel desperately needed a hero.

The Angel told Manoah's wife that their child would be special. Before he was born, she was not to drink any wine or strong drink, not to eat anything unclean, not even to eat any grapes or raisins. Her child was to do the same thing, and also he was never to cut his hair.

Manoah was not sure that the person who appeared to his wife was from God. He prepared a sacrifice and lit the fire to burn it up. When he did this, the Angel rose up to the heavens in the flames from the fire. Only then did Manoah know for sure that it had been an Angel who had appeared.

Manoah and his wife named their son Samson.

The Nine Choirs of Angels

THERE are different types of Angels. Over the ages, people have spoken of nine different levels, or choirs, of Angels.

The first two levels are Angels and Archangels. Angels are the type of Angels that we hear about most often. Archangels, on the other hand, are powerful messengers of God. There are three of them who appear in the Bible: Michael, Raphael, and Gabriel. Notice that all of their names end in "El." This is a Hebrew word that means "God," for all of the Archangels point to God.

We know little about the five choirs of Angels in the middle. They are the Virtues, the Powers, the Principalities, the Dominions, and the Thrones.

The highest levels of the Angels, the Cherubim and the Seraphim, appear more often in the Bible. These levels are immediately before God. According to tradition, Cherubim have four wings and Seraphim have six. We already saw Cherubim guarding the gates to Eden. For the Seraphim, we must look in the Book of the Prophet Isaiah.

Holy, Holy, Holy

ONE day, Isaiah received a vision of the holiness of God. He saw smoke rising up all around him, and he heard the Seraphim surrounding God singing,

"Holy, Holy, Holy,
Lord God of hosts,
heaven and earth are filled with Your glory."

We still sing this song during every Mass.

We sing "holy" three times for a reason. In Hebrew, the language that the people of Israel spoke in Old Testament times, there was no way of saying "more holy" and "most holy." In English, we can say, "big," "bigger," "biggest." In Hebrew, they had to say that something was "big," or "big, big" (for bigger), or "big, big, big" (for biggest).

By singing, "Holy, holy, holy," the Seraphim are saying that God is the holiest. All day long and all night long the Seraphim proclaim God to be the holiest One of all. There is nothing in the heavens or on the earth or even under the earth that comes close to the holiness of God.

The Archangel Michael

THE Angels we hear about most frequently in the Bible are the three Archangels: Michael, Raphael, and Gabriel.

Michael is called the prince of the Angels. He led God's forces against the forces of evil and thus chased Lucifer and the evil Angels out of heaven.

Even today Michael continues to battle against the forces of evil. He is a powerful defender of goodness and virtue and love.

The Book of Revelation speaks of this. It is a very difficult book to understand, but its message is filled with hope (for God will win in the end). In chapter twelve, we hear how Michael expelled the "accuser of our brothers and sisters out of heaven."

This accuser, Satan, points at each of us and reminds God that we are sinners. Yet, we are told that Satan is defeated by the Blood of the Lamb, Jesus. He does not want to condemn us. Jesus died for the forgiveness of our sins. That is why Michael chased the accuser out of heaven. God wants us to turn away from our sins and to accept His mercy.

The Archangel Raphael

ALL of the Archangels' names point to God's greatness. Michael's name means "Who is like God?" Raphael's name means "God heals." Gabriel's name means "God is a great warrior."

We hear about Raphael and his ability to heal in the story of Tobit. He was a good and virtuous man who always was careful to follow God's law and always wanted to help those in need. One day Tobit had the misfortune of falling asleep under a tree. A bird that was sitting over him dropped some of its waste into his eyes, blinding him.

Since Tobit could no longer earn a living, he sent off his son Tobiah to collect some money that he was owed. Raphael accompanied Tobiah on his journey and protected him. He even helped him meet Sarah, who would become his wife.

As Tobiah and Sarah were returning home, Raphael told Tobiah to go fishing. He caught a large fish, and Raphael told him how to make an ointment from some of the fish's inner organs. Tobiah rubbed this ointment on Tobit's eyes, and Tobit was able to see again, for God truly heals.

Gabriel and Zechariah

GABRIEL appears twice in the Gospel of Luke, both times to proclaim the birth of a child.

The first time that we see Gabriel he appears to Zechariah the priest. Zechariah was married to Elizabeth. They had grown old together, but they had never had any children.

One day, Zechariah was serving in the temple, and it was his time to perform the sacrifice. As he did so, the Archangel Gabriel appeared to him.

Gabriel told Zechariah that he should not be afraid, for God had heard his prayers. He and his wife would have a child whom they were to name John ("Yahweh is merciful"). This child was John the Baptist.

Zechariah was confused. He knew that he and Elizabeth were too old to have children, so he asked Gabriel how this could be. Gabriel revealed who he was and told Zechariah that he would not be able to speak again until his son was born. Zechariah had prayed for a child; yet when he was told that his prayers were answered, he could not believe it. Gabriel was telling him to be quiet and to meditate upon God's Word until it was fulfilled.

The Annunciation

THE next time that Gabriel enters the Gospel of Luke he appears to the Blessed Virgin Mary. We read there that Mary was betrothed to a carpenter named Joseph. This means that she was engaged, but they had not yet started to live with one another. Mary was a virgin.

Gabriel greeted her as one who was "full of grace." From the moment of her conception, God had protected her from every stain of sin.

Gabriel revealed to Mary that she would have a Child Whom she was to call Jesus, a name that means "Yahweh saves." Like Zechariah, Mary was confused. She was not yet married, and she had never been with a man. How could she have a Child? But Gabriel told her that the Holy Spirit would come upon her and she would have a Son, for nothing was impossible with God.

Here we see the difference between Mary and Zechariah. Zechariah had to remain silent to figure out what God wanted; Mary was ready in an instant. She responded, "I am the servant of the Lord. Let it be done to me according to your Word."

Angels Who Serve Jesus

ONE of the times that we do hear about Angels in the Gospels is after Jesus' temptation in the desert. He had gone there where He fasted for forty days and forty nights.

At the end of that time, Satan tempted Jesus three times to try to get Him to rebel against God the Father. Satan wanted Jesus to be selfish and to think only of Himself. He wanted Him to change stones into bread to satisfy His own hunger.

Jesus would not go along with what Satan wanted. He remained faithful to His Father and His own mission to save us from our sins.

After Jesus was tempted, we hear that God sent Angels to serve Jesus' needs.

Later we see an Angel during Jesus' time in the Garden of Gethsemane just before He died on the Cross. Jesus wanted to do the Father's Will, but it was going to be so difficult and painful to carry the Cross for us. God the Father sent an Angel in the garden to console and strengthen Him.

This is what the Angels do for us.

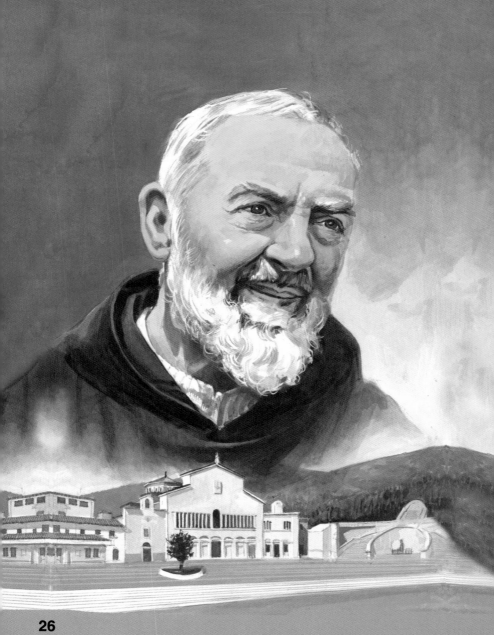

The Angels and the Saints

THROUGHOUT the history of the Church, we read many stories about Angels who consoled or challenged the people of God to do His Will.

During the Middle Ages, we hear about a young girl named Joan of Arc. She was poor and uneducated; yet Michael the Archangel appeared to her and told her to lead the armies of France to defend them against their enemies.

We also have a beautiful story about St. Francis of Assisi. A couple of years before he died, he went up on a mountain to pray in preparation for the feast of St. Michael the Archangel.

While praying, he had a vision of a Seraph Angel on a cross, who descended to him. After his vision, he had the five wounds that Jesus had on the Cross. We call these wounds the stigmata.

One of St. Francis's followers, St. Padre Pio, also had a strong devotion to St. Michael. He always recommended to people who felt tempted by the devil to pray to St. Michael because he would defend them against any temptation.

The Guardian Angels

BUT it is not just the great Saints who can talk to Angels. Every one of us has an Angel whom God has assigned to help and protect us from harm. It is our Guardian Angel.

Once, Jesus was speaking about how God loves and protects all of His people. He said, "Take care that you do not despise one of these little ones, for I tell you that their Angels in heaven gaze continually on the face of My heavenly Father."

In saying "little ones," Jesus was talking about little children, but He also was talking about those whom the world considers to be unimportant.

The Guardian Angels are the guarantee that God will care for us. The most important job of the Guardian Angels is to remind us of what God wants us to do—be generous, not selfish.

Once in a while, the Guardian Angels even protect us physically. People tell stories of how they were almost in an accident, or how they were very sick, and then something happened to protect them. Guardian Angels reached out to them.

Becoming a Messenger of God

WHILE Angels are totally spiritual creatures, there are ways that we can be like them. One way is to be unselfish and loving.

We can learn from their purity. Sometimes we use things in this world in a way that cheapens them. Perhaps we use and abuse our friends. Angels are single-minded and single-hearted. Love is at the center of who they are and what they do.

We can praise God for His goodness. God is great, and we should not be afraid to say it. Like the Angels, we can proclaim, "Holy, holy, holy."

We also can be messengers of God. The word Angel actually means "messenger." We have seen how they carried messages to people like Abraham and Sarah, Zechariah and Elizabeth, as well as Mary and Joseph.

We can be like the Angels by treating people with kindness and respect. We can act fairly toward them. We can give them a good example. Even though we cannot fly like the Angels, we can still be messengers of God's love.

A Prayer to Our Guardian Angel

THERE is an ancient prayer to our Guardian Angel that people pray each day. It is this:

O Angel of God,
my Guardian dear,
To whom His love
commits me here.
Ever this day,
be at my side,
to watch and guard,
to rule and guide. Amen.